W9-CPR-216

THE WAR IN KOREA

THE WAR IN KOREA

BY E. B. FINCHER

A GROLIER COMPANY

A FIRST BOOK
FRANKLIN WATTS
NEW YORK | LONDON | TORONTO | SYDNEY | 1981

32417
WILLISTON PARK PUBLIC LIBRARY

FRONTISPIECE: KOREAN CIVILIANS FLEE THEIR
HOMES IN A COMBAT ZONE AS U.S. TROOPS
MOVE TOWARD THE FRONT LINES.

Cover photograph courtesy of: United Press International

Photographs courtesy of: United Press International: pp.
ii, 13, 40, 47; World Health Organization Photo by Dale
Whitney: p. 6; National Archives: p. 14; Defense Depart-
ment Photo (U.S. Marine Corps): p. 24; Harry S. Truman
Library: p. 26; United Nations: pp. 32, 35, 43; U.S. Navy
Photo: p: 50.

Map courtesy of Vantage Art, Inc.

Library of Congress Cataloging in Publication Data

Fincher, Ernest Barksdale, 1910–
    The war in Korea.

    (A First book)
    Bibliography: p.
    Includes index.
    Summary: Describes major events of the war, includ-
ing events leading up to the war, parts played by signif-
icant leaders, and the war's outcome.
    1. Korean War, 1950–1953—Juvenile literature. [1. Ko-
rean War, 1950–1953] I. Title.
DS918.F53   951.9′042   81–2696
ISBN 0–531–04330–4   AACR2

Copyright © 1981 by E. B. Fincher
All rights reserved
Printed in the United States of America
6   5   4   3   2   1

CONTENTS

THE WAR IN KOREA

THE LAND OF
MORNING CALM

Washington was almost deserted that Saturday afternoon in late June. The capital looked so peaceful that it was hard to believe the nation was on the brink of war.

President Harry S. Truman was in Missouri, spending the weekend with his family. Secretary of State Dean Acheson, who directed foreign relations, was at his farm in Maryland. The secretary of defense and his chief military adviser were resting after a tour of duty in Asia. Other important government officials were vacationing far from Washington. As the lights went out in the capital on the night of June 25, 1950, the government of the United States seemed to close shop, like the stores downtown.

But not for long. From the other side of the world, messages were arriving that would rob many Americans of their sleep that night.

A foreign correspondent stationed in Seoul, capital of the Republic of Korea (ROK), notified his newspaper that the small nation had been invaded by a Communist force from the north.* His dispatch to New York was soon followed by an urgent message from the ambassador who represented the United States in the invaded country. This communication was directed to the State Department in Washington. Secretary Acheson was immediately notified of the threatening de-

---

Because the two countries are on opposite sides of the international date line (the mid-Pacific dividing line where the calendar day begins), Korean time is a day ahead of time in the United States. Thus the invasion began on June 25 Seoul time, but June 24 Washington time. Korean time is used in this book.

velopment in far-off Korea. Within minutes he had called several of his assistants and directed them to join him in Washington.

When the security telephone rang in President Truman's home in Missouri, he answered it himself. The secretary of state informed the President of the invasion of the Republic of Korea, a country that the United States had helped to establish and now protected. He told the chief executive that civilian and military officials were already conferring in Washington. Then the secretary asked for instructions.

The President realized that the invasion of the Republic of Korea threatened world peace. He said that he would return to Washington immediately in order to deal with the grave situation. The secretary of state persuaded him to wait until morning to leave Missouri. The secretary did not want President Truman to risk a hastily planned night flight to Washington. Besides, he told the President, the situation in Korea was still confused. By morning the picture would be clearer.

The President agreed to postpone his return. He instructed the secretary of state to call United Nations headquarters in New York, despite the lateness of the hour. The Republic of Korea had been set up by the United Nations, and any threat to its security was a concern of the world organization.

The chief officer of the United Nations, Secretary General Trygve Lie, grew alarmed when notified of the invasion. "This is war against the United Nations!" he exclaimed. He promptly began telephoning members of the Security Council, which is the peace-keeping branch of the United Nations. A meeting of the Security Council was scheduled for the next day, Sunday, to deal with the world crisis brought about by the invasion of the Republic of Korea.

While en route to Washington, the President conferred with the secretary of state from his plane by radio telephone, and summoned his civilian and military assistants to meet with him when he arrived in the capital.

The feverish activity in Washington and New York attracted the attention of scores of reporters for newspapers, radio networks, and television stations. Broadcasts describing developments in Korea caused many Americans to consult their atlases and encyclopedias. They wanted to locate the danger spot and discover why a small, distant nation could be so important to the United States.

THE SCENE OF WAR

Even a quick glance at a map of eastern Asia reveals why Korea is of great military importance. This thumblike peninsula belonging to the continent of Asia is a land bridge between the mainland and Japan, a nation of many islands lying offshore. The stretch of water separating Korea from the large islands of Japan is less than 150 miles (240 km) wide. Even before the days of battleships and landing craft, the strait was no great barrier to an invading force.

Because the strait was easy to cross, China and Japan through the years used Korea as a base for striking at one another, even though the peninsula is so rugged that it may be compared to a crumpled sheet of paper. Movement up and down the Korean peninsula was not confined to armies. Goods traveled overland to and from the mainland of Asia by that route. Equally important, ideas traveled in both directions. For example, China influenced the Japanese language and religion, as well as Japanese art, by way of Korea.

Further examination of the map of Asia shows why Korea is considered a danger zone. The country is surrounded by

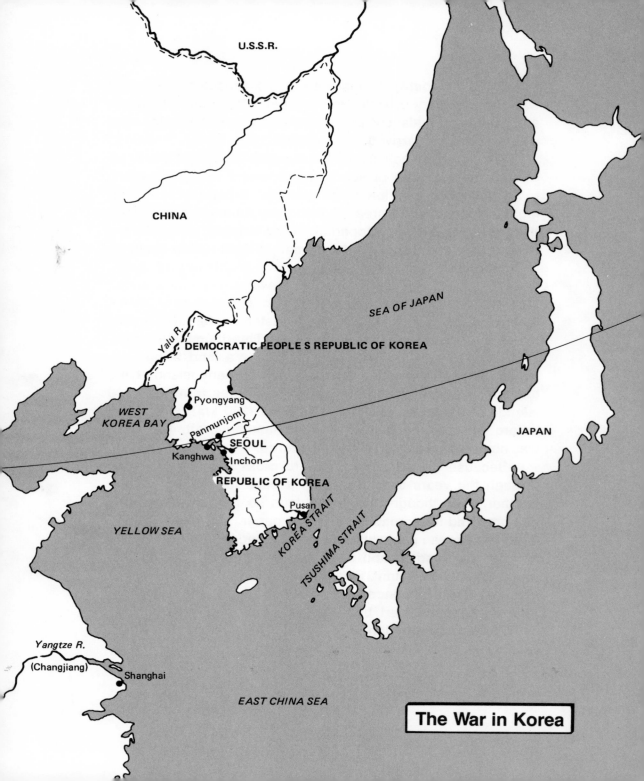

U.S.S.R.

CHINA

Yalu R.

DEMOCRATIC PEOPLE S REPUBLIC OF KOREA

SEA OF JAPAN

WEST
KOREA BAY

Pyongyang

Panmunjom

SEOUL

Kanghwa

Inchon

REPUBLIC OF KOREA

JAPAN

Pusan

YELLOW SEA

KOREA STRAIT

TSUSHIMA STRAIT

Yangtze R.

(Changjiang)

Shanghai

EAST CHINA SEA

The War in Korea

three of the most powerful nations in the world, China, Russia, and Japan. Their rivalry has often led to war, and Korea has been drawn into such conflicts because of its location. As we shall see, a fourth world power, the United States, became involved in Korean affairs when it occupied Japan at the end of World War II.

Korea, known to its own people as the Land of Morning Calm, has a history that goes back more than 3,000 years. During much of that time Korea was a kingdom that recognized the Emperor of China as its overlord. But despite their dependence on China, the Koreans had an identity of their own. Unlike the Chinese, the Koreans were very much alike in racial background, language, and customs. Moreover, their spoken language was very different from Chinese, and their written language was based on an alphabet instead of the thousands of ideographs, or symbols, used by the Chinese.

The Koreans were an inventive people who used movable type in printing before that system developed in Europe. One of their most famous inventions was a "turtle" boat—a warship covered with an iron shell that prevented it from being rammed or burned. With their turtle boats, the Koreans destroyed a large Japanese naval force that attacked their country in 1592—more than 250 years before the American ironclads, the *Merrimac* and the *Monitor,* fought their famous battle during the Civil War.

Like the Chinese and the Japanese, the Koreans had little contact with Europeans or Americans until the 1800s. Prior to that time, what direct knowledge the Koreans had of Westerners was gained from shipwrecked sailors or from Christian missionaries who entered the country secretly and were taken captive. Again like the Chinese and the Japanese, the Koreans considered foreigners to be uncivilized. Such barbarians were forbidden to enter Korea.

5

A traditional village in the rice paddies of Korea, the Land of Morning Calm.

The Koreans were even more determined to keep foreigners out of their country when they saw what was happening to their neighbors. Between 1839 and 1842, the British waged war against the Chinese. When the British won, they forced the Chinese government to give them trading posts along the coast. The French and other Europeans then demanded similar privileges. From these "treaty ports," Western influence spread across China.

In 1854, the American government opened Japan to world trade by sending a fleet to enforce its demands. The Koreans watched this shaming of another Asian nation and tightened their restrictions against foreigners. Christian missionaries from France who had entered Korea illegally were put to death. A French fleet sent to punish the Koreans in 1866 was destroyed. In that same year, an American merchant vessel, the *General Sherman,* defied the Korean ban on Western trading missions. The ship ran aground while moving up a river. The Koreans sent blazing rafts downstream and set the ship afire. What happened to the crew is not known for certain, but historians assume that all the sailors were put to death.

Alone among the Asian nations, Korea had managed to resist the West. But American manufacturers, like their European counterparts, were eager to sell their products to Korea, and American missionaries were eager to convert the Koreans to Christianity. So for various reasons, Americans turned to their government for help.

In 1871, President Ulysses S. Grant authorized the dispatch of a fleet to Korea. The naval force commanded by Rear Admiral John Rodgers was accompanied by Frederick Low, the United States ambassador to China. The purpose of this show of force was to persuade the Koreans to agree to a

7

treaty that would protect shipwrecked sailors. If possible, a treaty permitting Korean-American trade was to be secured as well.

Korean authorities ordered Admiral Rodgers to leave shortly after his fleet dropped anchor in their waters. The admiral replied that he would not leave until the Korean government agreed to a treaty. In the meantime, he proposed to have his crew survey the river that his ships had entered. He planned to make navigation charts that could be used by American merchant vessels.

The surveying party neared the fortified island of Kanghwa that guarded the approach to Seoul, the Korean capital. As the armed launches passed the island fortress, the Koreans opened fire. The Americans returned the fire with their vastly superior cannons. After silencing the Korean guns, the American force returned to the warships and reported to Admiral Rodgers and Ambassador Low.

The officer and the diplomat agreed that in firing on launches flying the American flag, the Koreans had insulted the United States. The insult would have to be punished; otherwise the American government would be disgraced.

Admiral Rodgers and Ambassador Low demanded an apology from the Korean authorities. They gave the Koreans several days to consider not only the required apology but also the matter of a treaty.

The Korean reply was not what the Americans expected. The defiant note stated that the Korean people "want nothing to do with you, or the rest of the outside world. We are content as we are. This is our right and our choice. Wherever you have gone, you foreigners have spread misery and unhappiness."

Several notes were exchanged before the admiral and

the ambassador realized that the Koreans had no intention of apologizing, much less agreeing to a treaty.

Admiral Rodgers gave the order for a full-scale attack on the island fortress that guarded the Korean capital.

The Koreans put up a determined resistance, but their ancient guns were no match for the modern cannons that blazed from the invading gunboats. After the American cannonade reduced the fortress, a landing party of sailors and marines came ashore with fieldpieces and ended Korean resistance by killing several hundred defenders. As the Americans withdrew, they blew up the fortress walls.

The destruction of the fortress did not produce the effect that the American command had expected. The Korean government not only refused to deal with the Americans, but it denounced them as savages.

Having failed in his effort to secure a treaty with the Koreans, Admiral Rodgers returned his fleet to its base in China. The expedition did not receive a commendation, as the admiral had expected. On the contrary, Admiral Rodgers and Ambassador Low were called before a committee of Congress when they returned to the United States. Several senators and representatives condemned the attack on the Korean fortress. As one senator said, the Korean expedition reflected no glory on the United States.

KOREA LOSES ITS BATTLE TO REMAIN FREE

The ill feeling against America that the attack on Kanghwa caused was soon pushed into the background by actions taken by Japan, an Asian neighbor of Korea.

Once Japan was forced to open its ports to world trade,

it quickly adopted Western ways. The Japanese army was reorganized and equipped with modern weapons. The Japanese navy was made into a formidable fighting force. In the meantime, Japan equipped its factories with machinery made in Europe and the United States. Once it became industrialized, Japan needed raw materials for its factories and markets for its manufactured goods.

It was not long before the Japanese showed an interest in the coal, and iron ore and other minerals known to exist in Korea. The great forests of northern Korea also attracted the attention of Japanese industrialists, and the rice fields of southern Korea were regarded as a source of food for Japanese factory workers.

Finally recognizing that it would have to yield to the superior force of Japan and the Western nations, Korea opened its doors to foreigners. The Japanese succeeded in making a trade agreement in 1876. Not long afterward, Korea made similar agreements with the United States and other Western nations.

Having secured a foothold in Korea through a trade treaty, the Japanese extended their control by waging war on China in 1894. The Koreans had long recognized China as their overlord. By defeating China, the Japanese removed one great rival. However, another rival soon challenged Japan for the control of Korea. Russia also had designs on what was once the Hermit Kingdom. The clashing interests of the Russians and the Japanese led to war in 1904.

Japanese soldiers moved north through Korea and China to strike at Russia. The invading troops were not withdrawn from Korea after Russia was defeated. Japan established a protectorate over Korea, which meant that in everything but name the peninsula became a colony. In 1910, Japan annexed Korea, thus making it an official part of a growing empire.

The Japanese developed Korean resources for their own use and discouraged the Western nations from trading with their colony. However, strong ties developed between Korea and the United States in one field—Christian missions. The treaties that Korea made with the Western nations permitted missionary activity, and Christians in the United States were quick to respond. American religious organizations sent missionaries to Korea to establish churches, schools, and hospitals. As more and more Koreans became Christian converts, they regarded the United States as a possible champion in their struggle against the Japanese.

The Koreans—Christians and non-Christians alike—suffered under the harsh rule of the Japanese. They were treated like a conquered and inferior people. The Japanese closed Korean schools as part of their effort to make their colonists forget that they once were citizens of an independent nation. A great deal of privately owned land was taken from the Koreans and given to Japanese settlers. All important positions in government and industry were occupied by Japanese. Books and newspapers were censored. The army and the secret police frightened most Koreans into accepting Japanese rule.

But thousands of Koreans fled their country to escape repression. Some of these refugees formed patriotic organizations in other lands and waited for an opportunity to restore the independence of their country. Among those refugees were two Koreans whose names were to become familiar to Americans in the years ahead.

One refugee, named Syngman Rhee, stirred up opposition to Japanese rule while a student in Seoul. He edited a newspaper that called for Korean liberation, led demonstrations against Japanese rule, and organized a secret patriotic society. Rhee was imprisoned as a revolutionist. When released, he came to the United States, where he studied at the universities of Harvard and Princeton. Later on he organized a Korean government-in-exile that would begin to operate once Korea regained its independence.

Kim Il-sung, who was to become Rhee's bitter enemy, fled to the Soviet Union to escape imprisonment by the Japanese. He graduated from a Russian university and became an officer in the Soviet army during World War II. Like Syngman Rhee, Kim Il-sung waited for an opportunity to make his country independent.

The defeat of Japan in World War II gave Korean patriots the opportunity they had been waiting for. At conferences held by British, Chinese, Russian, and American leaders during World War II, the Allies agreed to give Korea its independence. The United Nations, the world organization that had been established at the end of the war, made plans to hold elections that would bring the Republic of Korea into existence. The new republic would have the same boundaries as the old kingdom.

But a military arrangement made by the Americans and Russians during the final stages of the war prevented the fulfillment of the Korean patriots' dreams. The two allies agreed

In the south, Syngman Rhee was elected the first president of the Republic of Korea.

that after Japan was defeated, the Soviet Union would accept the surrender of Japanese forces stationed north of the 38th parallel. South of the 38th parallel, the United States would accept the Japanese surrender. (Parallels are the lines of latitude drawn on maps and globes to mark distances from the equator to the poles. The 38th parallel, which divided Korea, crosses the United States just north of San Francisco.)

What the American government regarded as a temporary military arrangement, the Soviet government regarded as the division of Korea into two countries—a Communist north and a non-Communist south. Representatives of the United States attempted to persuade the Soviet Union to permit the establishment of a united Korea. Having failed in that effort, American officials handed the problem of Korea over to the United Nations.

Kim Il-sung was chosen to head the government of the Democratic People's Republic of Korea in the north.

ONE PEOPLE—
TWO NATIONS

A Korean folk tale describes what happens to a shrimp caught between two whales that are fighting. The sad fate of the shrimp reminded Korean patriots of their country at the end of World War II. The rivalry of the United States and the Soviet Union had trapped Korea between two giants. The Koreans were powerless to unify their country until the "whales" agreed to it. And yet the Koreans were one people. They all spoke the same language and had the same customs. Their country had occupied the same peninsula for many centuries. They had made many sacrifices to regain their independence, only to be denied the right to set up their own government.

Koreans on both sides of the 38th parallel anxiously followed discussions between the Russians and the Americans. They read accounts of the debate on the Korean question at the United Nations. All the arguments put forward seemed to favor a united Korea.

To divide Korea into two countries would go back on promises made by the Russians themselves. Moreover, the division put both North Korea and South Korea at a disadvantage. The population was concentrated in the south, and that part of Korea produced most of the rice and other food eaten by the people of the entire peninsula. The valuable mineral and forest resources of Korea were concentrated in the north, and that area had most of the industries that the Japanese had developed during their occupation. The artificial boundary divided families no less than it divided resources. Trapped on both sides of the 38th parallel were Koreans who wanted to be reunited with their kin. They would never peacefully accept the division of their country.

The United Nations scheduled elections in both parts of Korea. However, the Russians refused to let United Nations officials enter North Korea. The election held in the area south of the 38th parallel resulted in the establishment (August 15, 1948) of the Republic of Korea, a nation about the size of the state of Virginia. Syngman Rhee was elected president of the new nation. Shortly thereafter the Russians set up the Democratic People's Republic of Korea, with Kim Il-sung as its premier, or chief executive. In size, North Korea was comparable with the state of Pennsylvania.

The disappointed and angry South Koreans (Republic of Korea) turned to the United States for support in their effort to reunite their country. The disappointed and angry North Koreans (Democratic People's Republic of Korea) looked to the Soviet Union and later on to Communist China to support their effort to control the entire peninsula. The 38th parallel became yet another boundary where the democratic nations and the Communist countries faced one another as enemies.

Both the North and South Koreans made military raids across the border that neither country accepted as permanent. Then on June 25, 1950, North Korea mounted a full-scale attack on South Korea in an effort to unite the two countries. The Korean War had begun.

"POLICE ACTION"
OR WAR?
As soon as President Truman returned to Washington from his home in Missouri, he met with his principal military and civilian advisers. The news from Korea was grave. The North

Korean Communists had crossed the 38th parallel with 90,000 soldiers, many of whom had been trained in the Soviet Union or Communist China. Leading the advance were 150 heavy tanks that the Russians had provided. The South Korean troops, whom the Americans had advised and supplied, had been trained more as a police force than as a regular army. The lightly equipped South Koreans fell back, unable to resist the tanks and heavy artillery of the invaders.

While President Truman and his advisers were planning the defense of the Republic of Korea in Washington, the Security Council of the United Nations was organizing support from its headquarters in New York. The Security Council first called for a cease-fire in Korea and a withdrawal of the Communist forces back across the 38th parallel. The Communists ignored the order. The Security Council then called upon all members of the United Nations to come to the assistance of the Republic of Korea.

Both as a member of the United Nations and as protector of the Republic of Korea, the United States attempted to halt the invasion. President Truman, as commander-in-chief of the armed forces of the United States, ordered air and naval support for the retreating South Koreans.

General Douglas MacArthur, who commanded American forces in the Far East, was placed in charge of the defense as head of the United Nations Command. From his headquarters in occupied Japan, he sent what forces were available to counter the North Korean attack. The defending army, reeling under the impact of tanks and heavy artillery, continued to retreat. Three days after the invasion was launched, Seoul—the capital of the Republic of Korea—was taken by the Communists.

At that point President Truman authorized General Mac-

Arthur to use United States ground forces in Korea. Since few American troops were available in the Far East, General MacArthur called for reinforcements from bases in the United States. While these military units were en route to Korea, American troops already in the theater of war joined with the South Koreans in trying to halt the Communist advance. At length, the defenders were driven south almost to Pusan, a port at the tip of the peninsula. There they made a stand.

To many military experts it appeared certain that the Americans would be driven from Korea. The peninsula at last would be united, and it would be under the Communist flag.

THE STRUGGLE FOR POWER

The conflict in Korea was regarded by students of world affairs as part of the global struggle known as the Cold War. On one side were the democratic nations of the world, led by the United States. Opposing them were the Communist countries, led by the Soviet Union. The conflict was the latest evidence that each group of nations was indeed afraid of the other.

The two armed camps developed as a result of World War II. A large part of the Soviet Union had been overrun by the German Nazis during that war, and millions of Russians had been killed or wounded. To protect itself from future invasions from the West, the Soviet Union set up a barrier by bringing the nations that bordered it under Communist control. First, the Soviet Union conquered Estonia, Latvia, and Lithuania and added the three small democracies to its territory. Then the Soviet Union forced the larger nations on its western border to accept the Communist system. East Germany, Poland, Czechoslovakia, Hungary, Bulgaria, and Rumania became Russian satellites, which meant that they were controlled by the Soviet Union. In a further effort to extend its influence, the Soviet Union aided the Greek and Turkish Communists in their unsuccessful attempts to gain control of those countries. On the other side of the world, the Soviet Union allied itself with mainland China, where the Communists came to power in 1949, the year before the Korean War began.

As American and Western European leaders watched the Soviet Union take over country after country, they became alarmed. It appeared that the Russians were determined to spread Communism to the whole world. It seemed that instead of merely trying to protect itself, the Soviet Union was waging a new kind of war against the democratic nations.

As leader of the free world, the United States responded to the Soviet Union's warlike moves with measures of its own. The democratic nations of Western Europe were provided with billions of dollars and extensive technical assistance for rebuilding industry, transportation networks, and other parts of their economies. In helping its allies to regain their industrial power, the United States was protecting Western Europe from Communist attack.

The barriers against the Soviet Union were further strengthened by a military alliance (North Atlantic Treaty Organization, or NATO) that the United States made with Canada and the democratic nations of Western Europe. To discourage the Soviet Union from bringing Asian nations under its control, the United States provided military and economic assistance to a number of Russia's eastern neighbors. The Republic of Korea was one nation that the United States aided in this manner.

The American military bases that ringed the Soviet Union and the People's Republic of China (mainland China) were established to prevent the further spread of Communism. The military bases were visible evidence that the United States had developed a policy of "containment" to halt Communist aggression. The fact that the United States was the only nation that had atomic weapons added to the feeling of security in the free world.

Then in 1949, the year before the Korean War began, news that the Soviet Union had exploded an atomic bomb sent shock waves around the world. The United States no longer had a monopoly on nuclear weapons.

When the North Koreans launched their attack on South Korea, it seemed to many Americans that the Communists were ready to challenge the United States in the Far East as they had in Europe. Certainly, President Truman and his advisers regarded the invasion of South Korea as a grave threat not only to the United States but to every non-Communist nation. For that reason, American officials called upon the United Nations to rally support among the free countries of the world. Meanwhile, the President and Congress began to mobilize, or put on a war footing, the economic and military power of the United States in order to block the Communists from further expansion.

The President described the defense of South Korea as a "police action," and Congress never declared war. But for all intents and purposes Congress and the President readied the nation for war. Many soldiers who had served in World War II were recalled, and young men were drafted into new armies. Warships were taken from "mothballs" where they had been placed at the end of the previous war. Factories turned from the production of automobiles and tractors to the production of tanks and planes. Just how quickly and thoroughly the mobilization of America took place can be shown in these figures: in 1950, before the outbreak of the Korean War, military personnel on active duty numbered 1,460,261. The year after the fighting began, the figure was 3,249,455.

THE SURPRISE ATTACK

The United Nations troops who were holding the Pusan area stood firm despite the waves of Communist soldiers that beat against the defense line. Meanwhile, troops, tanks, and artillery from the free world were arriving in Korea. The UN naval force established control of Korean waters, and the UN air force swept the skies.

After General MacArthur was placed in command of all UN forces, he planned what military experts describe as one of the most brilliant military campaigns in history. General MacArthur's plan for the landing at Inchon was inspired by General James Wolfe's attack on Quebec in 1759 during the French and Indian War. MacArthur recalled that the victorious British general struck the French at a point no one believed an army could attack. Caught off guard, the French were quickly overcome. The plan of attack that MacArthur worked out was as daring as the one used by Wolfe at Quebec.

The North Korean army had swept southward, and now it was battering the United Nations line near Pusan. To turn the military tables, MacArthur decided to make an amphibious, or land and sea, attack behind the North Korean force, cutting its supply lines and crushing it between his own troops and those of General Walton Walker, who was the commander defending Pusan.

The place that MacArthur chose to land his forces was the most unlikely point on the Korean coast. The entrance to the harbor of Inchon was narrow and defended by gun emplacements along the shore. But what made landing there so dangerous was the famous Inchon tide—one of the highest in the world. From low tide the sea rose 30 feet (9 m) and then quickly fell. Unless landing craft entered the harbor on high tide and speedily discharged their troops and equipment, the vessels would be stranded on mud flats when the tide went out. The landing craft would then be "sitting ducks" for enemy guns along the shore. To add to the danger of a landing at Inchon, seawalls lined the harbor. The attacking force would have to scale those high stone walls with ladders.

When General MacArthur explained the plan of attack to his officers, they were opposed. After considering all the dangers, one officer said that the general's plan had only one chance in 5,000 to succeed. But MacArthur was as persuasive as he was daring. He not only won over the officers who served under him, but he also secured the approval of the Joint Chiefs of Staff, the high command of the armed forces of the United States, based in Washington.

Before dawn on September 15, 1950, British and American cruisers and destroyers began to shell the shore batteries that defended Inchon. Then an air armada, or fleet, struck at the defenses. At high tide, landing craft entered the narrow channel and nosed against the seawall. Ladders were hooked to the top of the wall, and troops streamed onto land. By the time the tide rushed out, an entire army had been put ashore.

The attack caught the North Koreans completely by sur-

prise. Before they could organize a resistance, the UN forces had gained control of the port. Seoul, the South Korean capital, was soon recaptured, along with its important airport.

The effect of the Inchon landing quickly became apparent. The North Korean troops were cut off from their supplies when UN forces swept across the peninsula. Then the UN army that had been besieged in the Pusan area moved north to meet MacArthur's forces. The North Korean army fell apart, and more than 100,000 of its soldiers were taken prisoner.

Having cleared the invaders from South Korea, General MacArthur carried the war across the 38th parallel and captured Pyongyang, the capital of North Korea. He hoped to occupy all of North Korea before winter set in, when snow, bitter winds, and subzero temperatures would inflict heavy punishment on his troops. As the UN army neared the Yalu River, the boundary between North Korea and Communist China, spirits were high. Many soldiers believed that the war would soon be over, and that they would be home by Christmas.

The progress of the war was followed on military maps all over the world. As MacArthur moved his forces closer to the Yalu River, there was tension in Washington and alarm in the Communist capitals of the Soviet Union and China. The American high command realized that the Chinese Communists would become increasingly uneasy as a hostile army neared their border. For that reason General MacArthur was told to keep American troops away from the Yalu River. Only South Korean troops were to be allowed to advance that far.

U.S. Marines make a dramatic landing at Inchon, Korea.

Following the early victories of UN troops in Korea, President Harry Truman, left, *flew to Wake Island in the Pacific to meet with General Douglas MacArthur,* right.

Even before UN forces neared the Chinese-Korean border, the Chinese Communists warned via radio that they would not permit enemy forces to take positions along their frontier.

Syngman Rhee, president of the Republic of Korea, believed that his dream of a united and democratic Korea was about to be realized. For that reason, he encouraged his army to move forward.

General MacArthur refused to believe that the Chinese would carry out their threat to enter the war if UN forces reached the Yalu River. On November 20, 1950, UN troops advanced to the Chinese border. Six days later, they were attacked by 200,000 well-equipped Chinese soldiers who had crossed into North Korea. In less than a month, the Chinese army drove UN forces out of North Korea. Seoul fell to the Communists for a second time in January, 1951.

As General MacArthur studied the situation, he came to the conclusion that the war could be won only if the Chinese were forced to withdraw from Korea. And in his opinion, there was only one way to force withdrawal—Chinese military bases behind the Yalu River would have to be destroyed. That operation would require heavy air attacks on the People's Republic of China and possibly a naval blockade of the Chinese coast. Once Chinese military bases were destroyed, the invaders could no longer be supplied. Once its coast was blockaded, the People's Republic of China would be cut off from the rest of the world. The Chinese Communists would be forced to make peace.

General MacArthur's proposal to carry the Korean War into the People's Republic of China was laid before President Truman, the secretary of state, the secretary of defense, the joint chiefs of staff, and leading members of Congress. The proposal was studied from every angle before a decision was made.

General MacArthur was a respected commander. As a young officer he had a distinguished record in World War I. After peacetime service in the Philippines, he commanded the forces that defeated Japan in World War II. The general had then governed occupied Japan in a manner that was widely praised. His recent landing at Inchon had made him a popular hero in the United States, and a much admired military planner in other countries. Because of the general's standing, his request carried great weight.

THE GENERAL VERSUS THE PRESIDENT

The President, on the advice of his principal military and civilian advisers, turned down General MacArthur's request to carry the war into Communist China. He and his advisers noted that the commanding officer's plan failed to take several important facts into account. For one thing, General MacArthur was considering only the situation in Asia, where most of his life had been spent and where his great victories had been won. He regarded Communist China as the enemy, an enemy he felt confident that he could defeat if given permission to carry the war into its territory.

President Truman and his advisers saw the situation from a less narrow viewpoint. They felt responsible for the security of the United States and the rest of the free world. And they were more mindful of the Soviet threat should they take on China. They believed that if General MacArthur attacked Chinese bases, the Soviet Union would almost certainly come to the aid of its Communist ally. In all probability, the Russians would strike at Western Europe as the most effective way of assisting Communist China because the United States would then be forced to fight on two fronts. If the Soviet Union overran Western Europe, the United States would be in mortal danger. Moreover, the Korean War involved other members of the United Nations as well as the United States. Those members who were supporting the war effort made it known they were opposed to widening the conflict.

Faced with the prospect of World War III and the destruction of a large part of the human race by atomic bombs, President Truman directed General MacArthur not to carry the attack into Communist China.

The general considered the President's decision to be a grave mistake. He let his displeasure be known by protesting to some of his admirers in the United States. In a short time his views were made public by several members of Congress, certain newspaper editors, and other leaders who supported an attack on Communist China. Even after being warned that he was out of order in protesting the decision made by the military high command, General MacArthur continued to press for an attack on Communist China by air and sea.

MacArthur's conduct brought about a crisis in American government. According to the Constitution, the President is commander-in-chief of the armed forces of the United States. In other words, the Founding Fathers put a civilian in charge of the military establishment to safeguard democratic government.

As was pointed out by another famous general, George Marshall, then secretary of defense, it was MacArthur's privilege and his duty to make recommendations *before* the President reached a decision. It was not General MacArthur's right to take issue with the President's decision *after* it was made.

President Truman came to the conclusion that General MacArthur disagreed too strongly with the foreign policy of the United States and thus he could no longer be an effective commander. The President therefore removed General MacArthur from his post.

A wave of protest swept the United States. The dismissed general became the most popular man in the country. The President who dismissed him was denounced by many newspaper editors and threatened with impeachment by various members of Congress. When General MacArthur returned to the United States after an absence of almost fifteen years, he was given a hero's welcome. The United States Senate made a lengthy investigation of the dismissal. After the constitutional reasons for the general's removal were explained by a number of highly placed military and civilian witnesses, public opinion began to shift in favor of President Truman. Historians now defend the President's action and describe it as supporting an important constitutional principle—civilian control of the military establishment.

A NEW KIND OF ARMY

When General Matthew Ridgway replaced General MacArthur as commander of UN forces in Korea, he called attention to the international character of his army, which then had troops from sixteen nations. "I believe military history offers no parallel of so many allies serving side by side in battle so harmoniously—with such mutual confidence, respect, and cooperation." However, General Ridgway found that differences in religion and preferences in food presented some difficulties in this international army. The Dutch troops wanted milk, whereas the French wanted wine. The Muslim soldiers would not eat pork. The Orientals wanted more rice, and the Europeans wanted more bread. Shoes had to be extra wide for the Turks and extra narrow for the Filipinos.

Shortly after the change in the UN command, the Chinese and North Koreans began an all-out attack in yet another effort to bring the entire peninsula under Communist control. The Chinese used a plan of attack that was designed to undermine their opponents' will to fight. As General Ridgway described it, the Chinese favored moonlit nights for their attacks. First the artillery laid down a barrage, or wall of fire.

31

Moving at little more than arm's length behind the barrage came foot soldiers "hurling grenades without regard to losses. And again the wild bugles and barbaric screams sounded up and down the lines, while enemy infantry, padding silently up dark hillsides in rubber shoes, infiltrated our positions."

The UN forces withstood the all-out Communist attack. The Chinese and their Russian allies apparently realized that they could never win. On June 23, 1951, almost a year to a day after the North Koreans began the war, the Soviet spokesman at the United Nations proposed peace talks. Two weeks later, representatives of the contending armies met at a village near the 38th parallel to discuss a cease-fire.

But the fighting did not end for two more years. The Communists broke off peace talks several times and the conflict resumed. The type of warfare changed. During the first year of fighting, armies moved rapidly from one end of Korea to the other. For the next two years, the armies "dug in." War correspondents compared the type of fighting in Korea to the trench warfare of World War I. The Chinese entrenched themselves in the mountains by digging tunnels from one side to the other and then connecting the cross tunnels to make a network of passageways. Attacks were made from the tunnels, which were relatively safe from UN air strikes.

But even though there was less movement during the second stage of the Korean War, troops were still drenched

General Matthew Ridgway, center,
visits the Greek Battalion
fighting with UN forces in Korea.

by rain during the summer months as they slogged through the mud. In the winter months they were numbed with cold as they battled snow and ice. And while peace talks broke off, resumed, and broke off again, the death toll mounted.

As Americans fought under the UN flag in Korea, many changes were taking place in their home country. More and more young men were drafted into the armed forces and sent to Korea. Taxes rose as military expenditures climbed. The production of arms for Korea increased. In comparison, the production of goods for home use decreased. Because Americans were competing for relatively fewer products, prices rose. Inflation was the result.

The Korean War brought about several changes in American government. For one thing there was an increase in presidential power at the expense of Congress. In the previous conflicts in which the United States had engaged, Congress had declared war on the enemy nation at the outset. Congress had then shared with the President the responsibility for waging war. In contrast, President Truman called the Korean War a "police action," even though the full military power of the United States was engaged. Without asking Congress to declare war, President Truman mobilized the manpower and financial resources of the nation. Although the President called upon Congress to appropriate money and otherwise to support the war effort, he made the decisions. In the eyes of his critics, President Truman assumed authority that according to the Constitution belonged to Congress.

It was the Supreme Court, and not Congress, that successfully challenged President Truman during the Korean War. In 1952, Truman took control of the nation's steel mills to prevent a strike that he claimed would interfere with the war

Snow and bitterly cold weather made fighting more difficult for these Australian soldiers in Korea.

effort. The President explained the reasons for his action in a nationwide radio hookup and asked the American people to support him. He received little backing; instead, his seizure of private property was denounced by business leaders, newspaper editors, and many members of Congress. The steel companies took legal action to have their property restored, and the case came before the Supreme Court in short order. The high court ordered the President to return the steel mills to their owners. Truman promptly complied.

Some of the most important changes brought about by the Korean War were in attitude rather than substance. The fear of Communism became even greater when the Cold War between the free people of the world and the Communist nations gave way to actual combat. Congress passed laws restricting the freedom of speech, press, and assembly of American Communists. The legislation had the effect of discouraging anyone from criticizing the policies of the government. Senator Joseph McCarthy of Wisconsin accused scores of officeholders of being Communists or Communist sympathizers without any evidence to support his charges. Baseless accusations made by Senator McCarthy were also leveled at prominent people outside the government. Besides officeholders, many actors, writers, teachers, and artists lost their jobs because they were charged with being "un-American" or "soft on Communism." Some historians now use the word "witch-hunt" to describe the activities of Senator McCarthy and his supporters.

A FRIEND
BECOMES A FOE
It was difficult for many Americans to regard the People's Republic of China as an enemy nation when it first entered the

Korean War. Friendship between the Chinese and the American people had been a long tradition. More than a century before the Korean War, the United States had opposed the efforts of the other world powers to carve China into colonies, which had been the fate of many African and Asian nations. American educators, missionaries, and businesspeople had assisted China in becoming westernized. The United States had helped the Chinese to resist Japanese efforts to take control of their country. But after Japan was defeated in World War II, the United States continued to back the Nationalist Chinese in their struggle with the Chinese Communists. The Communists won the civil war, and they did not forgive the United States for trying to prevent them from coming to power. They regarded the United States as their chief enemy and were angry and afraid when its forces reached their frontier in 1950.

For its part, the United States feared the further spread of Communism in Asia. From the American point of view, the People's Republic of China menaced not only the Republic of Korea but also Japan, which the United States had promised to protect.

The American government used several means of checking the People's Republic of China. American military power was ranged against the Communist Chinese in Korea. The Seventh Fleet cruised off the Chinese coast, and vast military assistance was given to the Nationalist Chinese. These enemies of the Communists were established on Taiwan, a large island not far from the mainland. From that position they threatened to invade the People's Republic of China and destroy its Communist government. In a further display of its power, the United States blocked Communist China's efforts to become a member of the United Nations.

In the eyes of many Americans, their new enemy, the People's Republic of China, was the chief obstacle to peace in Korea. The North Korean representatives to the peace talks were unwilling to compromise because they had the backing of the Chinese army.

Peace talks broke down completely when representatives of the warring parties could not agree on conditions for releasing prisoners of war. The UN command held 75,000 North Korean and Chinese soldiers in its prison camps. The Communists had captured a much smaller number of UN soldiers.

Officers in charge of the North Korean and Chinese prisoners discovered that many of the captives did not want to return to a Communist country. Many of these soldiers had been forced into the army against their will. For that reason they asked to remain in South Korea when they were freed. The Communist representatives at the peace talks insisted that each North Korean and Chinese prisoner of war had to be returned to his own country, regardless of his wishes in the matter. The Communists did not want the world to know that thousands of their soldiers were unwilling to go home. Communist leaders claimed that life was better under their system of government than under any other. If Chinese and North Korean soldiers wanted to remain in South Korea, they would prove the Communist claims false.

Even though the disagreement over the release of prisoners prolonged the war, President Truman instructed American representatives not to yield. "We will not buy an armistice by turning over human beings for slaughter or slavery," he said. According to the President, the war was being fought to protect the democratic way of life. Even prisoners of war should be allowed the freedom of choice that democracy provides.

Changes of leadership in the United States and the Soviet Union speeded up the progress of peace talks in Korea. While campaigning as the Republican presidential candidate in 1952, General Dwight D. Eisenhower promised that if elected, he would make a trip to Korea in an effort to bring the war to an end. Eisenhower was elected and, before his inauguration, went to Korea to confer with the UN command. The President-elect encouraged its representatives at the peace talks to reach an agreement that would bring the long, bitter war to an end.

In the meantime the death of Joseph Stalin, the long-time ruler of the Soviet Union, removed an obstacle to peace. The new Communist leaders were more willing than Stalin had been to have the North Koreans reach a peace settlement.

Syngman Rhee, president of the Republic of Korea, was not allowed to participate in the peace talks. As the months passed, he became more angry and discouraged. He had spent his life working for the independence of Korea—a united Korea. He had seen his country devastated and hundreds of thousands of his people killed in a war brought on by rivalry between the United States and the Communist powers. Now spokesmen for those mighty nations were discussing terms of peace that suited them, not the Koreans.

Rhee had already made clear his own terms for peace— the withdrawal of Chinese troops from the entire peninsula, the unification of Korea, a defense alliance with the United States, and American economic and military aid. When he saw that the United States would not accept his conditions,

President-elect Dwight D. Eisenhower,
left, *visited troops at the war front*
on his trip to Korea in 1952.

Syngman Rhee almost wrecked the peace conference. He withdrew the ROK army from the UN command and released 27,000 prisoners of war that his troops had captured.

But the peace talks continued despite Rhee's opposition, and on July 27, 1953, an armistice was signed at Panmunjom by a representative of the United Nations and a representative of the Democratic People's Republic of Korea. A commission made up of representatives from Communist and non-Communist countries was made responsible for seeing that the terms of the agreement were carried out.

Although the fighting ended, the two Koreas did not make peace. They only accepted a cease-fire. The Koreans were more separated at the end of the war than they had been at the beginning. Kim Il-sung and his North Korean government discouraged all contact with South Korea. No trading could take place across the boundary, and there was no communication by telephone or mail. Many families that had become separated during the long war remained divided by the neutral zone created by the truce.

The cease-fire seemed to increase Syngman Rhee's determination to unite Korea. The vast military and financial aid given by the United States in the years following the armistice was used to expand and strengthen the ROK army. Increased military power encouraged Rhee to propose a new "drive to the north"—a campaign that never came about. Kim Il-sung, the North Korean strong man, was so feared and hated that the South Korean government rejected his suggestions that the two countries might be united by peaceful means rather than by renewed war.

COUNTING THE COST

The three-year Korean conflict was one of the most destructive episodes in history. Fifty-four thousand Americans lost their lives in Korea, and twice that number were wounded. Estimates of the cost of the war in dollars ranged from $67,000,000,000 to $164,000,000,000. The first figure was the estimated expenditure on the war itself. In arriving at the higher figure, experts added the estimated cost of providing veterans of the Korean War with various services during their lifetimes. These indirect costs of war included educational benefits, loans for housing, and medical treatment when needed. The second estimate of the cost of the Korean War also included the vast military and economic assistance given to the Republic of Korea as a result of the war.

Like the Americans, the Chinese paid dearly for their participation in the Korean War. Several hundred thousand Communist Chinese soldiers were killed or wounded in Korea. The People's Republic of China lost a large part of its best military equipment in supporting the North Koreans. The Chinese, along with the Russians, provided the North Koreans with

*A woman removes some rubble
from her stove in what remains
of her home in Seoul.
For the Korean people, the
effects of the war were felt long
after the fighting ended.*

arms during the war. After the fighting ended, both the People's Republic of China and the Soviet Union gave the North Koreans military equipment to match the arms that the United States supplied to South Korea.

But it was the Koreans on both sides of the 38th parallel who paid the highest price for the war. Five hundred thousand Koreans—a number approximating the population of Miami, Florida—were killed, and many times that number were wounded. In South Korea alone, 2,500,000 homeless refugees roamed about the country, and double that number were on relief. Most of the Korean peninsula was devastated. As tanks rumbled across the countryside, they ruined crops, damaged irrigation ditches, and brought down power lines. Bombers leveled cities and took out bridges. Ports were shelled by battleships.

The damage was not only to lives and property. When the war ended, Korea was still divided. Each country was dependent for its very existence on a more powerful nation. As a matter of fact, the North Koreans were dependent upon two powerful nations—the Soviet Union and the People's Republic of China. As long as the two Communist nations were allies, the North Koreans managed to keep on good terms with each of them. But when the Soviet Union and Communist China had a falling-out after the war ended, the North Koreans were caught between two powerful neighbors. This time, the "whales" were two Communist nations. The "shrimp" was North Korea. Trying to satisfy each of the rival nations that supported his country became one of the main tasks of Kim Il-sung, the leader of North Korea.

Syngman Rhee, president of the Republic of Korea, found it difficult to deal with the United States, the great power that supported his country. Rhee was seventy-three when elected president and seventy-eight when the war ended. A proud and independent man, he resented his complete dependence on American military and economic aid. This attitude often caused Rhee to be rude and overbearing in his dealings with American officials, some of whom came to dislike and distrust him. Rhee also angered many Koreans because he found it hard to share authority and to accept views that differed from his own.

Opposition to Syngman Rhee began to grow, particularly among high school and college students. They knew that many of Rhee's associates were dishonest, and that those Koreans were becoming rich at the expense of their countrymen. Moreover, Rhee's opponents believed that he should have made an effort to deal with the North Korean government instead of rejecting its offer to bargain. As opposition to Rhee increased, he bore down on his foes. Backed by the army and the secret police, he brought the legislature and the courts under his control. Freedom of speech and press were curbed, and leading opponents were jailed.

In 1960, when Rhee reached the advanced age of eighty-five, opposition to his harsh rule came to a head. Rhee stood for reelection that year, and his opponents claimed that once again the President had manipulated the election to his own advantage. When Syngman Rhee announced that he had received over 90 percent of the popular vote, a crowd of students estimated at one hundred thousand strong demonstrated against his government. The police fired on the demonstrators, killing and wounding several hundred of them.

The student rebellion received the active or silent support of most of the South Korean people. Everyone watched to see whether the army would crush the uprising. When the army refused to move against the students and their supporters, Syngman Rhee realized that his people had rejected him. On April 27, 1960, an era in Korean history came to an end. Syngman Rhee resigned as president and flew to exile in Hawaii.

THE BALANCE SHEET
The South Koreans got rid of one dictator only to have another come to power. The year after Syngman Rhee was overturned, General Park Chung Hee seized control of the government. For eighteen years, the general held South Korea in his grip.

Some Koreans opposed the one-man rule of General Park. But the new government won support from many Koreans because of the rapid improvement that Park made in living conditions. Drawing on the financial and technical assistance provided by the United States, the new leadership brought about what some experts called a miracle.

The hardworking, well-organized South Koreans quickly rebuilt their war-wrecked land. Seoul became a booming city much larger than Chicago. Its skyscrapers, subway system, and traffic jams gave it the appearance of a Western metropolis. The South Korean shipbuilding, electronics, steel, chemical, and rubber industries marketed their products throughout

General Park Chung Hee, right, visited President John F. Kennedy in Washington, D.C., to discuss U.S. aid for South Korea.

the world. Within a short time, the great majority of South Koreans could read and write, thanks to the system of required education. Meanwhile, the life of the average citizen was prolonged because of nationwide health care.

The South Koreans were justly proud of having built a prosperous country on the ruins of war. They enjoyed a living standard comparable to that of other industrialized countries. Their "success story" made the Republic of Korea an example for less developed nations to follow.

The advances made in South Korea contrasted with conditions across the 38th parallel. The North Koreans lived in a Communist country, which meant that they had less freedom than the South Koreans were given. In terms of length of life, education, and annual income, the average North Korean was behind the average citizen of South Korea. Although the population of North Korea (17,500,000) was less than half that of South Korea, its armed force was as large. In providing for its huge army, the Democratic People's Republic of Korea neglected its civilian population. But the powerful army enabled the North Korean government to menace its more prosperous neighbor.

In fact, the South Koreans lived in fear. Not far from Seoul, their capital, was the demilitarized (neutral) zone set up when the fighting ended. And just across this "no-man's-land," the North Korean army was concentrated. The North Koreans frequently violated the terms of the truce that ended the fighting. Armed bands raided South Korea, and gunboats made hit-and-run attacks on its coastal cities. From time to time, South Korean patrols discovered the opening of a tunnel that the enemy had dug beneath the demilitarized zone. The presence of these tunnels made the South Koreans dread surprise attacks along their boundary. Fear of such attacks was one reason for continuing military rule in South Korea.

While the people of South Korea enjoyed an improved living standard after General Park came to power, they were denied the right to speak and act freely. Park permitted no opposition to his rule. Officers of the numerous Christian churches, leaders of student associations, and labor officials were jailed and sometimes executed when they opposed General Park. Lawmakers and judges who questioned government policies were removed from office and often imprisoned.

TROUBLED TIMES

The South Koreans were always mindful of the hostility of the leaders of North Korea. In contrast, Americans tended to forget the Korean Communist army they had fought for three years. But on January 22, 1968, the people of the United States were rudely reminded that they had never made peace with North Korea. On that date, the North Koreans captured an American naval vessel. News that the *Pueblo* was in North Korean hands angered Americans, who stayed glued to their television sets to hear the details.

The *Pueblo* was equipped with highly sensitive electronic listening gear. Its mission was to cruise along the North Korean coast, monitoring onshore radio broadcasts and discovering the location of radar tracking stations. The information obtained by the *Pueblo* was used to locate North Korean military units and to break secret codes. In other words, the *Pueblo* was similar to the intelligence-gathering, or "spy," ships used by many major nations.

Since the *Pueblo* was a slow vessel and its three small guns were covered with canvas, it was not capable of resist-

The U.S. intelligence-gathering ship, Pueblo,
which was seized by the North Koreans in 1968.

32417

WILLISTON PARK PUBLIC LIBRARY

ing the fast, well-armed North Korean gunboats that surrounded it. The captain of the *Pueblo* radioed for help when he saw that the North Koreans meant to seize his vessel.

As soon as North Korean officers boarded the *Pueblo,* the Americans argued that their vessel was in international waters and therefore not subject to seizure. The North Koreans insisted that the *Pueblo* was in their national waters. Escorted by warplanes, the North Korean gunboats forced the American vessel into the nearest harbor.

The SOS that the captain of the *Pueblo* had sent to his base in Japan forced naval authorities to make quick decisions. The nuclear-powered aircraft carrier *Enterprise* was ordered to put about while en route to Vietnam from Japan. But the *Enterprise* never launched its planes, and fighter planes that had set out from Japan to rescue the *Pueblo* were ordered to turn back.

The *Pueblo* was taken as a prize by the North Koreans, and its crew was imprisoned for almost a year before they were released. The United States endured the situation for several reasons. Had attack planes been launched from the *Enterprise,* the crew of the *Pueblo* would have been endangered. Had the United States made an air and naval attack on North Korea to force the release of the *Pueblo* and its crew, the Korean War would have been resumed. President Lyndon Johnson and his advisers could not face that possibility. In 1968, the United States was fighting a desperate war with the Communists in Vietnam. It could not allow itself to extend that war to Korea. The *Pueblo* incident again reminded Americans that even though their country was among the most powerful in the world, there were limits to what it could do.

The day before the North Koreans were successful in

capturing the *Pueblo,* they were unsuccessful in an equally daring undertaking.

On a dark, bitterly cold night, a band of North Korean army officers disguised themselves as civilians. They cut the chain link fence that separated the two Koreas. When the soldiers felt sure that they had not been detected by an enemy patrol, they crawled through the fence and crossed the demilitarized zone into South Korea. They traveled by night and hid by day until they reached the outskirts of Seoul.

Their plan was to cross the city until they reached the Blue House, where General Park, the ruler of South Korea, lived. Using machine pistols and hand grenades, they intended to storm the Blue House and assassinate the South Korean leader. They believed that when Park died, the South Korean government would fall apart. Then Kim Il-sung, the leader of North Korea, could bring South Korea under his control.

None of the would-be assassins expected to survive the attack on the Blue House. They would be content to give their lives to help unite their country under the Communist flag.

The North Korean officers almost succeeded in their mission. They were in sight of the Blue House when the South Korean security police challenged them. The would-be assassins knew that they could not pass inspection, so they opened fire. The gunfire aroused the city. ROK soldiers and policemen surrounded the Blue House and then fanned out to capture the attackers. Within a few hours, all members of the assassination team had been killed or captured.

The attempt on General Park's life made the South Koreans more fearful than ever of their Communist neighbors. The general took advantage of this fear by tightening his control over newspapers, colleges, business and social organizations, and other possible sources of opposition to his rule. His grip on Korean affairs was then almost complete.

Having seized power as an army officer, Park made himself the lawful head of the government by forcing his election as president of the Republic of Korea. Once securely in control, Park had the Korean constitution changed so that he could stay in office as long as he chose and rule as he pleased.

Even though the Korean people had not succeeded in setting up a democratic government, many of them still refused to accept dictatorship. They resisted General Park as they had resisted Syngman Rhee. Despite the efforts of the secret police to prevent Park's opponents from organizing, students defied the law and demonstrated against the government. Carefully hidden printing presses continued to turn out anti-Park leaflets that were widely distributed. One of the general's opponents attempted to assassinate him but killed his wife instead.

It was not one of the general's political enemies who brought his rule to an end but a high-ranking member of his government. In October 1979, General Park was assassinated by the head of the South Korean secret police.

The army officers who took control of the government immediately placed the nation under complete military rule. In establishing martial law, the army officers made opposition to their rule even more difficult than it had been under General Park. Public demonstrations were outlawed; newspaper, radio, and television reports required government approval; those who criticized government policies were jailed. Although they placed further restrictions on the freedom of South Koreans, the military rulers promised to hold elections once order was restored.

Such promises became meaningless when one of General Park's supporters secured enough backing in the army to make another change in government. General Chon Too Hwan forced the leaders who had taken control when Park was assassinated to retire from office. General Chon then assumed command of both the military intelligence agency and the civilian military agency. As head of the two secret police forces, General Chon became what American journalists described as "South Korea's new strongman."

Although the new leader seemed to have almost total control of his country, foreign observers pointed out problems that might bring about his downfall. The great prosperity that South Korea had enjoyed during General Park's rule was brought to an end by a worldwide economic downturn. As prices rose and employment declined, more and more Koreans became dissatisfied with their government. Despite all efforts to frighten students into accepting military rule, young Koreans continued to wage massive demonstrations against the government. And older Koreans who had devoted their lives to opposing dictatorship continued to resist the new strong man as they had resisted earlier ones.

To further complicate General Chon's problems, the matter of unifying the two Koreas came up again in 1980. Across the 38th parallel, the North Korean army continued to face the South Korean forces. At any moment, the uneasy truce made in 1953 might be broken and the war resumed. The assassination of General Park and the upheaval caused by his death provided the North Koreans with an opportunity to invade the Republic of Korea with considerable chance of success. And yet it was during the upheaval that the governments of the two Koreas agreed to discuss the unification plan that had been dropped many years before.

No one familiar with the Korean War and its aftermath expected quick results from such a meeting. The two Koreas are still suspicious of one another. But in the opinion of some experts on Korean affairs, the proposed meeting was a hopeful sign that leaders in the two countries believe the time has come to write the last chapter in the history of the Korean War.

WARS BEGIN MORE
QUICKLY THAN THEY END

The Koreans were not alone in wanting an end to war. Decades after Americans became involved in hostilities in far-off Korea, they still had heavy responsibilities in that country. American troops continued to serve in Korea on a rotating basis to keep the United States military force at full strength. When successive Presidents proposed to reduce and eventually remove American military personnel from Korea, there were always strong objections. South Korean leaders wanted American troops to remain as a safeguard against another invasion from North Korea and as a warning to the Soviet Union.

Not only were American troops still based in Korea almost thirty years after the war supposedly came to an end, but the South Korean army was still advised by American officers and still equipped by the United States. The close ties between the South Korean and the American military forces aroused opposition in certain quarters in the United States as well as in South Korea. Critics in both countries agreed that if the United States government did not give strong support to Korean dictators they could not stay in power. According to this view, American officials could force Korean strong men to give their people more freedom by threatening to withhold military and financial aid.

Since the South Korean government was highly dependent on the United States, its officials attempted to influence Congress and the president to act favorably on its requests. In their efforts to influence American policy, South Korean officials sometimes resorted to dishonest practices. In 1976, for example, a Washington newspaper uncovered a scandal that brought to light many illegal connections between agents of the South Korean government and members of the Congress of the United States. The Justice Department, which is the law-enforcement division of the federal government, and a committee of the House of Representatives conducted investigations of the relations between ROK agents and American officeholders.

The investigations showed that South Korean agents had attempted to influence Congress by offering some of its members campaign contributions or outright bribes. Other members of Congress were given free trips to Korea or were entertained at a fashionable Washington club that was owned by a Korean businessman who had close ties with his government. The same businessman arranged for several members of Congress to share in the profits of questionable deals between American companies and the South Korean government.

As a result of the investigations, several members and former members of the House of Representatives were brought to trial and others were reprimanded by Congress. By the time the well-publicized investigations and the trials came to an end, many Americans were aware of yet another result of their country's involvement in the Korean War.

An important change in American military policy can be traced to that same war. As noted earlier, President Truman used the term "police action" to describe the kind of war that he conducted in Korea. Truman and his advisers also developed the idea of "limited war" during the conflict. In other words, instead of fighting total, "no holds barred" war with its enemies, the United States restricted the Korean War to a certain area and to certain weapons. In this respect, the Korean War differed from World War I and World War II, which were global wars, and in which the United States and its enemies used all the weapons available to them.

The Korean War was confined to a relatively small peninsula. The United States did not attack Chinese military bases nor blockade the Chinese coast. Although North Korea had Russian backing, the United States did not strike at the Soviet Union. And even though the United States had an arsenal of atomic weapons, they were never used against the North Koreans and their Chinese allies. In short, President Truman and his advisers developed the idea of limited warfare as a means of preventing World War III, a global war that would probably destroy the human race.

Since 1950, the year the Korean War began, Americans have discovered that strong, and sometimes unwanted, ties have developed between their country and the Republic of Korea. But the Korean people are far more conscious of these ties than Americans are. For one thing, South Koreans feel that their safety depends upon the presence of an American military force and on the military equipment that the United States provides the ROK army, navy, and air corps. The South Koreans also are mindful of the fact that the United States has given or lent their government hundreds of millions of dollars. Moreover, the United States provided technical assistance when South Korea began to Industrialize, and once its factories produced goods, Americans became important customers.

Less noticeable than these physical indications of American influence are the great changes that have taken place in Korean attitudes since 1950. Contacts between American military personnel and the South Korean people have popularized Western ways. The hundreds of thousands of American servicemen and -women who have been stationed in Korea have introduced the people of that country to chewing gum, blue jeans, rock music, cowboy movies, and other aspects of American culture. The free-and-easy and free-spending Americans have made the South Koreans feel that the United States is a rich, democratic country—in fact, something of an earthly paradise.

This view of the United States has caused the young people of South Korea to demand from their government more freedom to rule themselves, along with an opportunity to enjoy the high standard of living that they associate with the United States. Discontentment with their lot has caused some South Koreans to attempt to change their government. Discontentment has made other Koreans anxious to leave their country and come to the United States.

A survey recently made by a leading newspaper in Seoul showed that 50 percent of the people of the Republic of Korea want to leave their country. Most of those who would like to emigrate regard the United States as the country to which they would most like to go. Since the United States restricts the number of future immigrant citizens to 290,000 each year from all countries, few South Koreans can fulfill their dream.

Each year only about 25,000 South Koreans are admitted to the United States as future citizens. But already small communities of South Koreans have begun to form in major American cities. The presence of these groups of Korean-Americans is further evidence that what began as a border war in a country remote from the United States has brought changes that will influence American life for generations to come.

FOR FURTHER READING

Allen, Richard C. *Korea's Syngman Rhee*. Rutland, Vermont: Charles E. Tuttle, 1960.

*Berger, Carl. *The Korea Knot*. Philadelphia: University of Pennsylvania Press, 1964.

*Chung, Kyung Cho. *Korea: The Third Republic*. New York: Macmillan, 1971.

Detzer, David. *Thunder of the Captains*. New York: Thomas Y. Crowell, 1977.

Fehrenbach, T. R. *This Kind of War*. New York: Macmillan, 1963.

————. *The Fight for Korea*. New York: Grosset & Dunlap, 1969.

Gosfield, Frank, and Bernhardt J. Hurwood. *Korea: Land of the 38th Parallel*. New York: Parents' Magazine Press, 1969.

Heinl, Robert D. *Victory at High Tide*. Philadelphia: J. B. Lippincott, 1968.

*Heller, Francis H., ed. *The Korean War: A 25-Year Perspective*. Lawrence, Kansas: The Regents Press of Kansas, 1977.

*Jackson, Robert. *Air War over Korea*. New York: Charles Scribner's Sons, 1973.

Lawson, Don. *The United States in the Korean War*. New York: Abelard-Schuman, 1964.

Leckie, Robert. *The War in Korea, 1950–1953*. New York: Random House, 1963.

*McGovern, James. *To the Yalu*. New York: William Morrow, 1972.

Ridgway, Matthew B. *The Korean War.* Garden City, New York: Doubleday, 1967.

Solberg, S. E. *The Land and People of Korea.* Philadelphia: J. B. Lippincott, 1966.

*Wade, L. L., and B. S. Kim. *Economic Development of South Korea.* New York: Praeger, 1978.

Werstein, Irving. *The Trespassers.* New York: E. P. Dutton, 1970.

* For more advanced readers.

INDEX

WILLISTON PARK PUBLIC LIBRARY

T 15373

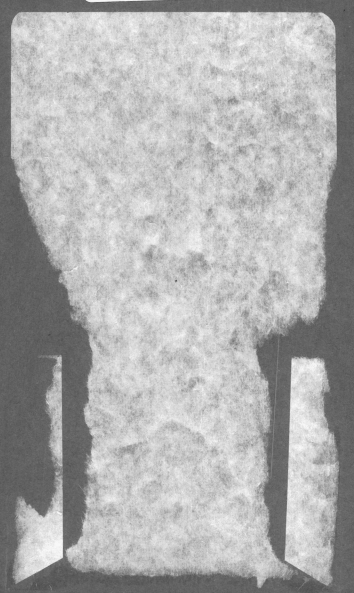